My Humble O

Novels by Paul Connolly
(also featuring Lundy Island)

The Fifth Voice
The Enduring Influence of Ken Potts

'*A delight, full of wonderful descriptions of settings and
weather... gives the reader a feel for this unspoiled island*'
TripFiction

'*Emotionally intelligent... you get absolutely caught up*'
Devon Life

'*Painted with extraordinary skill*'
Tim Brooke-Taylor

'*Connolly writes with insight and authority*'
Bristol Post

'*A fabulous book... thanks for enriching my life*'
Richard Campey

'*After we met in the Lundy pub garden, I bought your first
book and loved it!*'
Sharon Critchlow

'*I read the first Lundy chapter and realised I could trust you
on the rest. Absolutely loved it... finished it with a smile on
my face and a tear in my eye*'
Ruth Waterton

'*The details about the island are accurate... and also the
magic*'
Laurence Glazier

My Humble Observatory

Paul Connolly

Rocket Pole

Published by Rocket Pole Press
www.rocketpolepress.com

ISBN: 978 1 65558 110 6

British Library Cataloguing in Publication Data
A CIP catalogue record for this book is available
from the British Library

Cover and interior illustrations based on original
photographs by Paul Connolly

For Georgie, Joan, Robin, Helena, and Harriet

*Old God sure was in a good mood
when he made this place*

Hunter S. Thompson, *The Rum Diary*

.

CONTENTS

Lundy

Ageless rock
You are an ocean jewel
A permanent place of peace and magic
That draws me back time and again
To replenish my spirit, to nourish my soul

Westerly wild
Easterly calm
Your unspoilt grace is Nature's balm

I tread upon your ground
In the footsteps of pirates and prisoners
And touch shipwrecked souls
On pitch black nights
When the wind and rain drive hard and unforgiving

Then in summer
When your rare gifts blossom
You sparkle bright and pure
Bathed in panoramic azure hues
Light everywhere, a painter's dream

Westerly wild
Easterly calm
Your unspoilt grace is Nature's balm

I miss your magic when I am away
But it comes to me now and then
A voice in the night, a beacon of light
Wight, Portland, Plymouth
Biscay, Fitzroy, Sole
Lundy

Westerly wild
Easterly calm
Unspoilt grace, Nature's balm

A Moderate Crossing

Sea conditions are described as moderate
Said the captain's voice
As the Oldenburg reversed in Ilfracombe harbour
While people settled in their seats
And Verity, upright and exposed, waved farewell

Twenty minutes later
The boat was being tossed about on waves
In a scene from *Moby Dick*
And though I thought I knew what moderate meant
Modest, medium, middling this was not

Soon people were turning pale
Not so talkative as before, some lying down
And then the crew started to weave expertly around the deck
Handing out paper bags
Vomit duty a routine part of the job

One by one, passengers succumbed
Copiously relieving themselves of their breakfast
Or straining as their stomachs heaved but yielded nothing
But the acrid sting of bile inside their throats
All the while trying to breathe deeply

Not for me this sickness, I thought
As I stood with both hands gripped to the rail of the deck
Feet wide apart, sight fixed firmly on the horizon

As the biggest swell took my innards by surprise
And I grabbed a paper bag – just in time

Landing At Jenny's Cove

Two hours, the standard crossing
Turned into nine
No jetty to moor up to
And a contrary wind that wouldn't relent
So at last the captain decided
To land at Jenny's Cove

The Oldenburg dropped anchor
On the west side of the island
Spilling its human cargo like seabirds home to roost
And with climbing ropes as guides
Boat and island staff helped everyone to the top
Young, old, fit, and not so

Impossible to imagine in these days of Health & Safety

Arrival

Stepping off the Oldenburg
And the first footfall catapults me into my alternative world
Where the past doesn't matter
The future matters less
And the present hugs me like a long-lost friend

Hello again beach road
Hello again great green beauty
I can't wait to sink into your landscape
Lose myself in your rock and gorse and bracken
And render myself insignificant in your magnificence once
more

The Climb

Down the galvanised metal gangplank
Along the wooden boards of the jetty
Past the dive shed, gas cylinders, rope coils
Towards the road, hugging vertical cliffs
Pinned and secured by giant rusting bolts

The road twists and climbs steeply
My head drops, my body leans in, my heart thumps
Behind me, below me now, on the rocky beach
A solitary seal basks, unconcerned by the human influx
While down on the jetty a tractor loads cargo from the boat

The road turns in towards sparse woodland
A freshwater stream gurgles somewhere unseen
And from the canopy of branches comes birdsong
As the cream-painted face of Millcombe House
Nestles in the crook of the valley, peeking through

And on to a set of carved stone steps
That lead to a still higher path
The final lung-busting ascent to the top
Where, as I gasp for air
I can't stop myself from smiling

Marisco Tavern

No colourful emblems or crests
No crowns, lions or stags
Proclaim this beating heart of the island
Just a simple painted signboard announces
Marisco Tavern

Wooden-clad bar room, flagstone floor
Walls festooned with flotsam and jetsam
Lifebelts, ensigns, ship's bell
The wreckage of yesteryears
Paying tribute to lost souls

Rock climbers circumnavigate the centre table
Divers share stories of Montagu and Karksburg
Birdwatchers hope for rare sightings
Children play Jenga and Scrabble
Lovers discover new romance

Sustenance after long walks
Old Light and Experience
Sharing discoveries, listening to the day's tales
Fingers on the pulse of the island (the beating heart of the
    island)
Marisco Tavern

Preparation

Table pushed against the window
Chair and cushion in place
A tractor trundles down towards Brambles and rounds the
    bend
A birdwatcher stalks through the bracken below
A dive boat waits in the bay beyond
A couple carry provisions over the hill to Hanmers
A light wind ruffles the long grass outside

Laptop, check
Notebooks, check
Binoculars, check

I free my mind of the mainland
Lift the lid of the laptop
And begin

When The Lights Go Out

Scrabble players miss their triple-word score
Jigsaw pieces fall to the floor
Trump cards hover, frozen mid-hand
As darkness makes its swift demand

Words go unspoken as sentences pause
And drinkers spill wine onto living room floors
While books fall from hands and go the same way
When the lights go out at the end of the day

Midnight on Lundy, that magical hour
Plunged into darkness, drained of all power
Everyone stumbles to bed in no doubt
That at midnight on Lundy the lights go out

The Walls Have Eyes

Shipwreck, mutiny, danger at sea
Rain lashing, sails thrashing, skulduggery
Gigantic waves, smugglers' caves
A transatlantic fleet
These are the things that look down from the walls
Of your Lundy Island retreat

Storms, tempests, gale force winds
The ultimate sailor's fright
These are the things looking down from the walls
In ominous black and white

But look again and you'll see
The odd piece that's twee
A basket of fruit or a flower
A fisherman's net, a jelly just set
Or a damsel distressed in a tower

And this juxtaposition
Is not meant as derision
It's there for your personal delight
To bring a smile to your face
As you stumble or race
To the loo, with your torch, in the night

Picnic At Benjamin's Chair

On the wall of Big St. John's
Four women, three men pose stiffly for the camera
Against a backdrop of granite over a hundred years ago
The women looking down or to the side
Modesty forbidding eye contact with whoever might gaze
    upon their faces
The men looking straight into the lens, inviting the onlooker
    to admire their worth
One with a cocksure stare, a shotgun slung over his shoulder
Commanding the scene
A frigid family scene
A scene called *Picnic At Benjamin's Chair*
A picnic without food or drink
Or joy of any kind
As far as I can see
A creepy old photograph that could easily be
The centrepiece of a Stephen King story

Small Things

Listening to silence
Breathing fresh air
Watching the sun rise over the sea
While drinking tea

Enjoying the weather
Whatever the weather
Wind and rain hammering at night
Fog enveloping everything in sight

Tracing the arc of a rainbow
Or the gentle glide of a gull
Spotting a ship as it comes into view
Clouds parting, revealing blue

The chattering of starlings
A scattering of sheep
A basking seal in the Landing Bay
Shimmering light on a hot day

Checking the time on the church clock
And being none the wiser
Tea and biscuits after a walk
Feeling no necessity to talk

Reading a book in the Tavern
While draining a glass to the dregs

Then ordering another
And another

On the island I take great pleasure in small things

The Haunting

In the still of a stifling July night I trudged
Sweat-soaked, from bed to bathroom once again
In the grip of some abdominal turmoil
And in my delirium, as I edged through the darkness
I sensed that I was not alone

In the living room, I felt a palpable presence
And my heart froze as ghosts appeared
Lining the walls of Square Cottage
My hands reached in front of me to keep the ghosts at bay
And in my fear, despite my fear, I needed to know my fate

'Who's there?' I asked at last
At which the presence shifted and moaned
Then spoke to me, chilling me to the bone
'It's Us,' came a voice
'Who? Who are you? What do you want?' I gasped

'The tent blew away, so we let ourselves in,' came the voice
of my sister

St. Helena's

South of the village, dominating the skyline
St. Helena's stands alone, a bleak Victorian monument
A huge granite house in praise of God

The clock on the tower's eastern face tells three o'clock
By chance, the time of the crucifixion
Depicted in bright stained glass within

And carved into the sandstone pulpit
'Thy Word Is A Lantern Unto My Feet'
Gives meaning to readings so rarely heard

While from the lectern, an ornate eagle prepares to fly
As words once flew from the mouths of preachers
Touching congregations before soaring heavenwards

This place of praise stands empty and forlorn
Except on days when its great bells peel, stirring past glories
A ringing reminder of the grandeur of St. Helena's

The Baptism

He stood on the threshold of Government House
A biblical apparition with beard and staff
Come to calm the souls of the island's newest visitors

PJ, island chaplain, over from Appledore
Eyed the playing infants
And saw an opportunity crawling before him

Peering over the top of his Old Chelsea Ironstone teacup
He quizzed 'Have these children been baptised?'
And upon the answer 'No'
He smiled and suggested (though it seemed more like a
    command)
'St. Helena's, 2pm, Tuesday'

And so Georgie and Helena came to be baptised
Numbers thirty-seven and thirty-eight in the registry
Welcomed into the family of the church
And given the life-long gift of Lundy

Lost Love

You danced a sailor's hornpipe near North Light
Then walked precariously on the edge of Devil's Limekiln
As changeable as the island weather
One minute calm and bright
The next tempestuous and dark
But then I didn't know you held a secret

When later your secret was out
What love we had
Like ill-fated ships cast upon unseen rocks
Was lost
And in my desperation, I almost lost myself
But for the comfort of
Landing Beach
Devil's Kitchen
Rat Island
Old Light
St. Helena's
Marisco Tavern
Earthquake
Gannets Bay
North Light
Jenny's Cove
Quarter Wall
Halfway Wall
Three-Quarter Wall

I thank them all
For helping me survive lost love

Top & Back

Leaving the shadow of St. John's Valley
Checking the church clock to see what time it isn't
Risking a broken ankle at the cattle grid
Walking through the village not knowing if the shop's open
Counting the tents in the camping field
Wondering what goes on in the work sheds
Stopping to watch starlings plump and shimmer in the eaves
Eyeing the line of dry stone wall as its granite glints
Smiling as Gloucester Old Spots shuffle and shunt in mud

On to Quarter Wall as ravens swoop and perch
Where ponies slowly graze
Following the standing stones as the road winds
Past the hollow remains of Quarry Cottages
Through unfurling bracken and yellow gorse
Past Pondsbury and the red, brown and yellow of cattle
    lazing

Then on to Halfway Wall and halfway there
Past Tibbets, wondering if anyone is staying
Taking in the big sky at Three-Quarter Wall
Onward until the scrub wears thin
And the surface rock shines white
The road narrowing, undulating
Scruffy Soay scurrying
Goat horns silhouetted against the western sun
And then at last a sense of getting there

As the road peters out at the thin end

The top end

Where the only way is back

The Old Light

Two hundred years ago
The Old Light was built on the highest point of land
Tall, proud, and implausible
Its lantern five hundred feet above sea level
A towering white elephant made of granite

Two hundred years ago
The Old Light, island icon, dominated the landscape
Standing with its head in the clouds
The opposite of what it was meant to be
A hazard to shipping

The Blue Bung

Six granite steps and a corrugated carapace of blue
The Old School nestles against the battlement wall above St.
 John's Valley
A colourfully conspicuous feature of the gentle Eastern
 slopes
An escaped parakeet
A painter's aberration in a moment of frustration
A tin-pot, dare-to-be-different dwelling
An iron and timber anachronism

The one-time Sunday school, one-time drinking den
This cobalt curiosity
Looks out across the sea and boldly suggests
Come be my guests
Step into the Blue
You know you want to

A View From Hanmers

Looking down upon Rat Island
Snowy spume dashing against the dark rock
In the foreground, the jetty
Skeletal, quiet, expectant
And beyond, countless waves rise and fall
Tearing bone-white slashes
In the broad green canvas of the Bristol Channel

The wind whips northwards
Driving banks of cumulus cloud
That throw shadow cloaks upon the sea's green
And then, within seconds, the clouds thicken
And all is grey, as dense rain falls and swirls
Shrouding everything in sight

A minute later
And the clouds shift once more
Parting this time to allow bright blue patches to appear
As though an unseen artist
Was adding the final touches of colour
To a painting entitled 'A View From Hanmers'

Curse Of The Letter R

Why does Lundy have a curse on the letter R?

Rats
Rabbits
Rhododendrons

Has anyone seen Reg today?

The Man Who Shall Not Be Named

On the island over forty years
The man who shall not be named
Has never let his photograph be taken
And yet his stories fill the place
Of Gade and Harman and beyond

Watching everything from his corner
The man who shall not be named
Talks of maids and matelots he has known
Every face, every place
Recalled with perfect clarity

For fear of offending
The man who shall not be named
I'll say no more than this
No photographs will identify him
But maybe, just maybe, these words will

The Shooters

'Buffalo Bill's back'
Said the man who shall not be named
As the Shooters appeared
All tell-tale camouflage and scabbards

The Shooters, after a day's shooting
Settled down to an evening's talk of shooting
Soay, deer, the regular cull
And then the Shooters were hungry

'What's on special? I could eat a horse'
Said one of the Shooters
No horse, but Soay stew
Venison sausages, steak and kidney pie

And after careful deliberation
The armed and camouflaged man made his choice
Vegetarian bake
With garlic mushrooms to start

Fancy Dress

Unaware that New Year's Eve was fancy dress
We had to improvise
Four of us went as zombies
One as the world's most famous boy wizard
The undead covered their faces in ash from the hearth
Hollowed their eyes with charcoal
Applied red lipstick where blood was needed
While the boy wizard
Found round glasses and a robe
Was etched with a lightning bolt
And came armed with her Nimbus 2000

Unsurprisingly, no prizes for the flesh eaters
But when the children's prize was announced
And my young niece was thrust into the spotlight
The poor thing burst into tears
Clinging tightly to the spoils of victory
A large tin of Quality Street
Which she later stored for safety under her bed
The lid intact for the rest of our stay
Despite the best efforts of the revenants
An impressive feat of magic
From young Harriet Potter

The Iron Figure

Looking out from Stoneycroft
Across the green swathe towards the South West point
Where the island gives way to the squall of the Channel
    beyond
I see a solitary figure standing resolute against the elements
Just visible through a familiar hanging mist
And as I walk towards the figure, expecting movement, there
    is none
It stands sentinel, solid, stoic
It will be there night and day, through battering winds and
    rain
And then again when the sun blazes upon its cubic form,
    casting shadows
But only for a year
I wonder, is that time enough for the island to permeate its
    ferrous skin
And imbue it with the same sense of wonder I feel every
    time I'm here?

Fresh Eyes

Previously my only brush with ornithology
Was on a university field trip many years ago
In a Devon woodland we wore magnets on our heads
An experiment in avian migration
After that nothing
After that not so much as a passing curiosity
After that ornithological oblivion

Then one day on the island
I opened my eyes to the skies
Opened my ears to the wind
And suddenly it was different
Until then our feathered friends were invisible
Until then birdwatchers were weird
Until then binoculars were a weight around my neck

My first sightings were a revelation
Sparrow, starling, swallow
And the next, majestic
A kestrel, hovering, hunting
Now I see it
Now I get it
Now I have fresh eyes

The Beast From The East

When the Beast from the East came calling
The island sat in the eye of a storm
Battered by a polar wind
Fierce and lacerating
Driving snow hard across the Channel

When the Beast from the East came calling
A boat was swept aground and made matchwood
Water pipes froze and burst
The generator failed
And snow drifted under the door

When the Beast from the East came calling
I fixed blankets against the door
Retired to bed mid-afternoon with hot water bottles
Wearing three pairs of socks and a fleece
While the snow painted white fractal patterns at the windows

When the Beast from the East came calling
The walk to the Tavern was an arctic expedition
Trekking through the white out
Fighting the Beast as ice crystals razored my face
Slicing, exfoliating

When the Beast from the East came calling
And I was cosy by the Tavern fire
One of very few who ventured out

It occurred to me that discretion was the better part of valour
So I borrowed a walking pole and went home before it was
    too late

A Spoiling Fog

In the sparse timber confines of the embarkation shed
The air crackles as a gaggle of travellers giggle and cavort
Like children away from home for the first time
Each one rainproofed and backpacked
Ready for the seven-minute ride
While outside a spoiling fog hangs

A walkie-talkie sparks up, cuts through
Reporting no improvement yet
If it doesn't clear by noon, no flights today
And the air crackles a little less
As some turn thoughts to Plan B
While others sit quietly and hope
That the spoiling fog lifts

Meanwhile, on the island
Departing visitors pack the Tavern, awaiting news
Some stare out to sea, dreaming
Others stare at the fire, worrying
Each one rainproofed and backpacked
Ready for the seven-minute ride
While outside a spoiling fog hangs

A high-vis jacket walks from office to bar
Reporting no improvement yet
If it doesn't clear by noon, no flights today
As the dreamers dream of another long walk

And the worriers reach for their mobile phones
No one quite knowing
If the spoiling fog will lift

The Big H

Huddled near the Big H
Shivering in a bitter south-westerly
Wind sock at full stretch
Fire truck standing by
The next seven leavers gather for final instructions
And decide who sits next to the pilot

Looking above the roofline of the black shed and church
High up in the blanket grey sky
A small dot appears then grows
Its sound repelled for now as the wind blows hard
And one of the seven gets special instructions
How to ride shotgun on her birthday

Then the sound cuts through, intermittent at first
The tell-tale thrum of rotors growing louder
As, with insect grace, the sleek machine descends
Lowers, hovers, tacks against the wind
Tips its nose in greeting
Then settles softly down against the Big H

Ground crew move quickly for the switch
The quad bike tows luggage fro and to
Arrivals emerge, ducking and shuffling to the track
Then the leavers follow signals to replace them
As the rotor blades thrash, the engine changes pitch
The machine lifts and spins, then angles sharply away

My Humble Observatory

I stand stock still
Head raised in awe at the ink black sky
And the myriad stars that jostle for position
Each one a pin-point reminder of how small we are
How little we know

And this, my humble observatory
Puts Greenwich and Jodrell to shame
For surely the outside urinal on Lundy Island
Has the best view of the universe in the world

To find out more about Paul Connolly's writing and to contact the author, visit www.paulconnollyauthor.com